Gordon Simm
and
Jacquetta Megarry

Rucksack Readers

Cleveland Way: a Rucksack Reader

Published in 2012 by Rucksack Readers, Landrick Lodge, Dunblane, FK15 0HY, UK

Telephone +44/0 1786 824 696

Website ***www.rucsacs.com***

Email info@rucsacs.com

ISBN 978-1-898481-55-3

British Library Cataloguing in Publication Data: a catalogue record for this book is available from the British Library.

Designed in Scotland by **WorkHorse** (***www.workhorse.co***)

Printed in England by Ashford Colour Press on water-resistant, biodegradable paper

Publisher's note

All information was checked prior to publication. However, changes are inevitable: take local advice and look out for signage e.g. for diversions. You are advised to check the official website for updates before setting out: ***www.nationaltrail.co.uk/clevelandway***

The weather in north-east England is unpredictable year-round, and parts of the Way are exposed, remote, and wet underfoot. You are responsible for your own safety, and for ensuring that your clothing, food and equipment are suited to your needs. The publisher cannot accept any liability for any ill-health, accident or loss arising directly or indirectly from reading this book.

Feedback is welcome and will be rewarded.

We are grateful to readers for comments and suggestions. All feedback will be followed up, and readers whose comments lead to changes will be entitled to claim a free copy of our next edition upon publication. Please send emails to **info@rucsacs.com**.

Cleveland Way: contents

Foreword

Of Britain's many fine National Trails, the Cleveland Way is one of the oldest and most popular. It opened in 1969, only four years after the Pennine Way, and it has delighted walkers with its variety and challenges ever since. All of us who walk it today are indebted to its pioneers: see page 61.

This is also the National Trail with the strangest shape – a lopsided horseshoe. It sets out westerly from Helmsley past Rievaulx Abbey and the White Horse of Kilburn, swings north along the Hambleton Hills to Osmotherley, then heads north-east through the Cleveland Hills past Captain Cook's monument and over Roseberry Topping, undulating all the way to the Victorian resort of Saltburn by the Sea. Here it changes direction, heading decisively south-east via the historic towns of Whitby and Scarborough, to finish at the headland of Filey Brigg – thereby ending about 30 miles east of its start!

It is also two trails in one. There is the inland Way that skirts the North York Moors, an enormous expanse of heather moorland and a National Park, with panoramic views from the escarpment over the vales of York and Mowbray and many chances to enjoy wilderness wildlife. And then there's the coastal Way which follows this heritage coastline with its undulating cliffs, fishing villages, smugglers' coves and North Sea views. Separately, each of these is over 50 miles. Together they form an epic journey of 108 miles (174 km) through an extraordinary range of scenery, heritage and human history.

East towards Carlton Moor

Which direction?

The route comprises two contrasting sections: the inland section runs between Helmsley and Saltburn by the Sea and it's better to walk that long section of 56.5 miles (91 km) from south to north, putting the prevailing south-westerly winds behind you on the exposed moorland. Most people follow on with the coastal section, a further 51 miles (82 km) from Saltburn to Filey, generally south-east. On trend, however, that can mean heading into the wind. If splitting the walk into two, there's a case for reversing direction on the coastal section, starting instead at Filey and walking north-west to Saltburn. Scenically this works well, culminating with a walk over the east coast's highest cliffs near the end, and you'd spend your final night at the splendid town of Saltburn.

The Tabular Hills Walk (THW) is a 48-mile waymarked route that links the coast near Scarborough to Helmsley. To some walkers, this is the missing link that bridges the gap between the Cleveland Way's start and near-finish, simplifying logistics because you can embark on the loop at any point. To others, at 108 miles the Way is already long enough, and extending it to 156 mi/251 km unthinkable. The THW begins near Scalby (see page 56, bullet 6) and the Long Distance Walks Association provides information on this route which is shown on Ordnance Survey mapping: see pages 61 and 62.

This book confines itself to the main Way, and follows the generally preferred direction, starting from Helmsley and ending at Filey. However, route-finding along the coast is mostly very straightforward, and the mapping is readily usable either way. Whether you complete the route in a single expedition or split it into several, spend some time planning where to break your stages, whether to walk in company or alone, and how to handle accommodation and baggage.

Some walkers opt for the services of a holiday company to make some or all of the arrangements – accommodation, baggage transfer and transport to the start and from the finish. Others prefer to make their own choices. You will find links to holiday companies from the websites listed on page 62.

What is the best time of year?

For most people, the best time to walk the Cleveland Way is between May and September, although March/April and October also have some good periods of weather. November to February is generally not recommended, unless you live locally, can go at short notice on a good forecast and are aware of the implications of very limited daylight.

In summer, you're likely to enjoy better weather, you'll have a greater choice of accommodation and are certain of longer hours of daylight. This is important not merely for covering the distances safely, but also for having time to make side-trips. More castles, abbeys and refreshment stops will be open in season, and public transport is also more frequent.

How long will it take?

Most people take nine or ten days to cover the full distance (108 miles/174 km): see Table 1 for two ways of breaking the route down. Part 3 of this book is divided into nine sections, with an average of 12 miles (19 km) a day. For some walkers, each is a feasible day's walk, but for others the 17-mile stretch between Saltburn and Sandsend will make too long a day: they should consider either splitting it at Staithes or using a different 10-day breakdown as shown in Table 1.

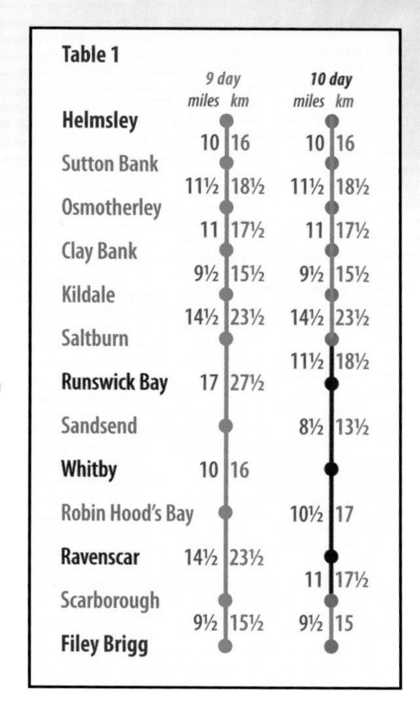

Table 1

Stage	9 day miles	9 day km	10 day miles	10 day km
Helmsley – Sutton Bank	10	16	10	16
Sutton Bank – Osmotherley	11½	18½	11½	18½
Osmotherley – Clay Bank	11	17½	11	17½
Clay Bank – Kildale	9½	15½	9½	15½
Kildale – Saltburn	14½	23½	14½	23½
Saltburn – Runswick Bay			11½	18½
Saltburn – Sandsend	17	27½		
Runswick Bay – Whitby			8½	13½
Sandsend – Robin Hood's Bay	10	16		
Whitby – Ravenscar			10½	17
Robin Hood's Bay – Scarborough	14½	23½		
Ravenscar – Scarborough			11	17½
Scarborough – Filey Brigg	9½	15½	9½	15

In general, the Way is blessed with plenty of accommodation that is either on or very close to the route, but inevitably you will walk much further than 108 miles in the daily process of reaching food, drink, accommodation and making side-visits. You also need to allow travelling time at either end; and you may wish to add a spare day for bad weather or to take a break from walking.

Unless you are an experienced walker, avoid committing yourself to long daily distances. Not only do you risk turning your holiday into an endurance test, but also time pressure may make you miss out on side-trips that would have helped you to understand the history and heritage of the places you pass through. Even the placenames are full of local interest: see page 62 for the meanings of some Yorkshire words.

If you have little or no previous experience of long-distance walking, please obtain our *Notes for Novices*: see page 63. In addition to advice on footwear and other gear, it explains factors affecting daily distance.

Terrain and gradients

The terrain varies from field paths to moorland tracks and minor roads, with quite a few steep flights of steps, short stretches of sand and, to combat path erosion from heavy footfall, some stone-paved sections. In general, the Way has good going underfoot, with occasional muddy parts which can be very boggy after prolonged rain and in winter. Although the Way never rises above 454 m (1490 ft), it undulates quite a lot, not only over the North York Moors but also along the coastal sections. Don't expect rapid progress in the undulating sections: see the altitude profile below.

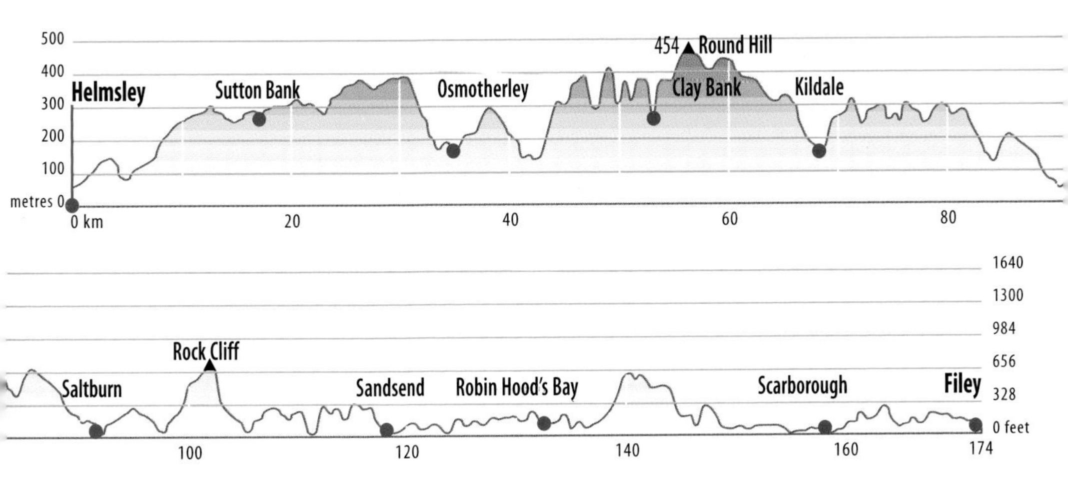

Tides

At Runswick Bay (shown below), there's a short stretch of beach which it's normally easy to walk across but in stormy weather or at extreme high tide may pose an obstacle. To check on this ahead of your walk, visit ***easytide.ukho.gov.uk*** and check the data for Whitby – which is near enough. High water times are always given in Greenwich Mean Time. Between the last Sunday in March and last Sunday in October, add one hour for British Summer Time.

Waymarking

The route is clearly waymarked throughout its length, often by name but sometimes just with the National Trail acorn logo: see the illustration. Since it doesn't intersect or overlap with any other National Trail, always follow the acorn. In particular, if you see a marker with more than one arrow, always follow the one nearest to the acorn. For example, this marker post means 'Bear right to follow the Cleveland Way, bear left to follow a different public footpath'.

Countryside Code and dogs

Please follow the Countryside Code as revised in 2012: see page 62.

Think hard before deciding to bring your dog on the Way. Unless you are camping and eating outdoors, there are many places where you might wish to eat or sleep where your dog won't be allowed. Some B&Bs accept dogs, others impose extra cleaning charges, restrict dogs to 'very well-behaved' or refuse them altogether: ask before booking. There may also be dog issues while on the walk, especially where livestock are in fields and your dog must be kept under close control. Always clean up after your dog if it soils the path.

Travel planning

There are airports at Newcastle, Teesside (renamed "Durham Tees Valley") and Leeds/ Bradford. Mainline railway stations are at Leeds, York, Malton, Thirsk, Northallerton and Middlesbrough. North Sea Ferries serve Hull and take passengers by bus to Hull railway station for travel to Scarborough by train then to Helmsley by bus; and between Hull and Filey by train or bus. For transport and weather websites, see page 62.

Coastliner bus services from Leeds connect to Pickering via York and Malton, and to resorts on the east coast. Other buses connect Helmsley with York, Malton, Scarborough and Middlesbrough.

Many small towns on or near the Cleveland Way are connected directly by rail, including Saltburn, Great Ayton, Kildale, Whitby, Scarborough and Filey.

Bus services from Malton and Scarborough serve southern parts of the region, and from Whitby serve the coast and northern parts. As of 2012, coastal bus travel is easy, with frequent services between Middlesbrough, Whitby, Scarborough, Filey and Hull. However, more careful planning is needed to reach Helmsley and Sutton Bank, especially in low season – and on Sundays it may be impossible. In summer, however, daily buses ply between Helmsley and Sutton Bank, with a useful hourly service.

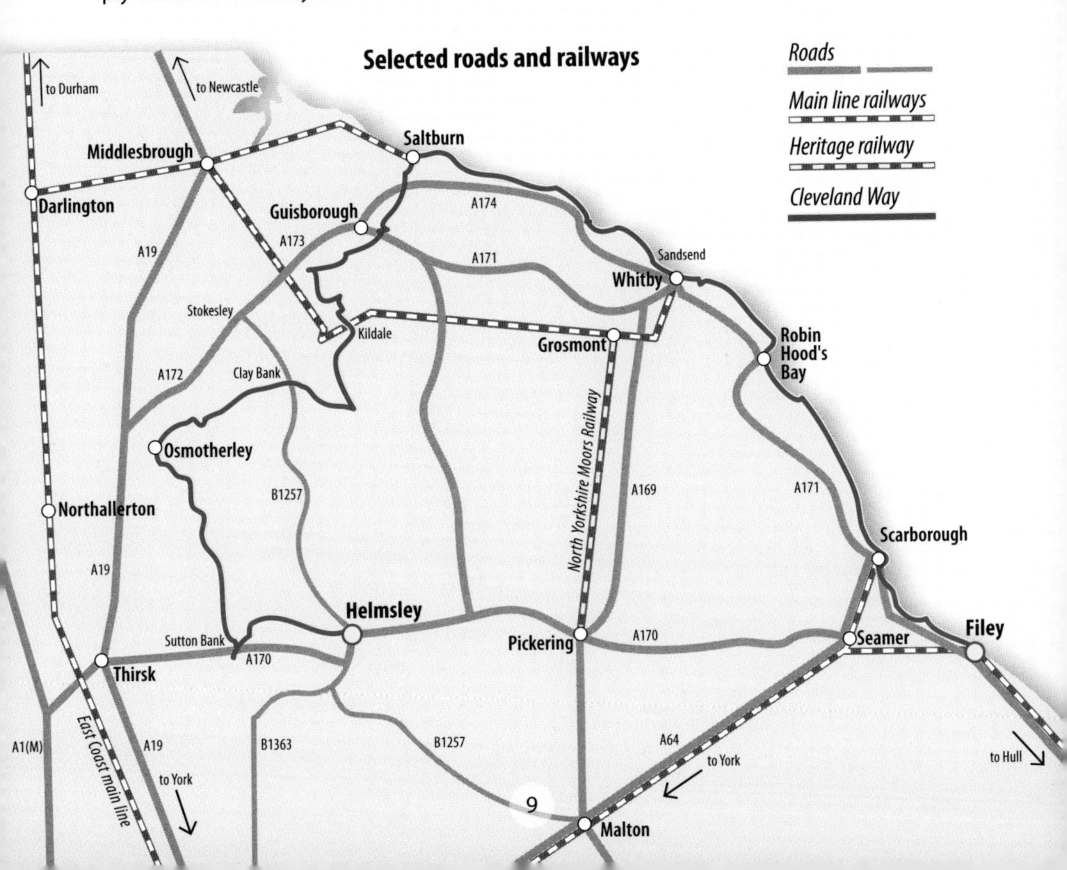

Accommodation

The Cleveland Way has a good range of accommodation, from campsites, bunkhouses and hostels through to farmhouse B&Bs and hotels both small and grand, mostly on or very close to the Way. Download the official *Accommodation & Information Guide*: see page 61. Our table on page 11 provides an overview of options as of April 2012: note the caveat at foot of page.

Don't be misled by the apparently wide choice: you need to book well ahead of your walk if you want a soft bed. Along the coastal section it's normally easy enough, but the inland sections cross sparsely populated moorland. For example, there are no B&Bs at Clay Bank (but some in Raisdale, Bilsdale and Great Broughton) and only one near the Way at Kildale (albeit another one 2 miles offroute at Percy Rigg, transport by arrangement).

Many B&Bs are small and some get fully booked far in advance. Others charge hefty supplements for single occupancy, are closed out of season or are merely in the wrong location for your itinerary. Some B&Bs offer lifts by arrangement, indicated by a car symbol in the official download. Before relying on this, check and discuss timing. Mobile phone signals can be patchy, so never depend on a last-minute phone call.

Hostelling deserves special mention because the route was originally devised to link Youth Hostels (see page 61) although some have since closed or moved. As of 2012, there are hostels at Helmsley, Osmotherley, Whitby, near Robin Hood's Bay and near Scarborough. It's important that walkers make good use of them, and hostels have reinvented themselves for the 21st century to offer some privacy and comfort at modest cost. The old days of austerity and excessive rules are long gone. Nor do you need to carry sleeping bag liners, just a towel.

If you are camping, you have huge flexibility at the price of carrying heavy loads. Alternatively you can use a baggage service – in which case you lose most of the flexibility, because you still have to book the pickups and drops. But it is certainly the lowest cost approach.

Maltkiln House, Bilsdale

Facilities along the route

	miles from last place	km from last place	café	pub	shop	campsite	hostel, barn, bunkhouse	B&B, hotel
Helmsley			✓	✓	✓		✓	✓
Cold Kirby	5½	8·9						✓
Kilburn 1½ mile				✓				✓
Sutton Bank / Hambleton	4½	7·2	✓	✓		✓		✓
Osmotherley	11½	18·5	✓	✓	✓	✓	✓	✓
Carlton Bank (Lord Stones)	7½	12·1	✓			✓		
Beakhills Farm ⅔ mile						✓		✓
Clay Bank	3½	5·6						
Great Broughton 2 miles				✓	✓	✓		✓
Chop Gate/Bilsdale 2 miles				✓		✓		✓
Kildale	9½	15·3	✓				✓	✓
Great Ayton 2 miles			✓	✓	✓			✓
Guisborough 2½ miles			✓	✓	✓			✓
Slapewath	10	16·0		✓				✓
Skelton Green	2¼	3·7		✓				
Skelton	½	0·8	✓	✓	✓			✓
Saltburn	2	3·2	✓	✓	✓			✓
Skinningrove	3¾	6·0	✓	✓	✓			
Staithes	4¾	7·7	✓	✓	✓	✓		✓
Port Mulgrave	1½	2·4	✓	✓				✓
Runswick Bay	1½	2·4	✓	✓		✓		✓
Sandsend	5½	8·9	✓	✓	✓			✓
Whitby	3	4·8	✓	✓	✓	✓	✓	✓
Robin Hood's Bay	7	11·3	✓	✓	✓	✓		✓
Fylingthorpe ½ mile						✓		✓
Boggle Hole	1	1·6					✓	
Ravenscar	2½	4.0	✓			✓		
Hayburn Wyke	4¼	6·8	✓	✓				✓
Scalby Mills	5¼	8·5		✓		✓	✓	
Scarborough	1½	2·4	✓	✓	✓			✓
Cayton Bay	5	8·0				✓		
Filey	4½	7·2	✓	✓	✓	✓		✓

Table correct at time of publication: some facilities are available only in season. All details should be checked before making plans that depend on them. Places that are offroute are shown in italics with distance after placename.

Packing checklist

The checklist below refers to your daytime needs, and is divided into essential and desirable. Experienced walkers may disagree about our categories, but this list makes a starting-point. Normally you will be wearing the first three or four items and carrying the rest in your rucksack.

Essential

- comfortable, waterproof walking boots
- specialist walking socks
- breathable clothing in layers
- waterproof jacket and over-trousers
- hat and gloves
- guidebook, map and compass
- in case of injury, whistle and torch for attracting attention
- water carrier and plenty of water (or purification tablets/drops)
- enough food to last between supply points
- first aid kit including blister treatment
- toiletries and overnight necessities
- insect repellent and sun protection (summer)
- rucksack (at least 35 litres)
- waterproof rucksack cover or liner, e.g. bin (garbage) bag
- enough cash in pounds sterling, with credit/debit card as backup.

Credit cards are not always acceptable and cash machines are sparse along the Way. Bin bags have many uses e.g. store wet clothing or prevent hypothermia.

Desirable

- walking pole(s)
- binoculars: useful for navigation and spotting wildlife
- camera (ideally light and rugged), also spare batteries, memory card or film
- pouch or secure pockets, to keep small items handy but safe
- gaiters (to exclude ticks, as well as mud and water)
- toilet tissue (biodegradable)
- small plastic bags for litter
- spare socks: changing socks at lunchtime can relieve damp feet
- spare shoes (e.g. trainers, crocs or sandals)
- towel if hostelling
- notebook and pen
- mobile phone: useful for arrangements but don't rely on one for emergencies. Reception can be patchy.

Camping

If you are camping, you need much more gear, including tent, sleeping gear, camping stove, fuel, cooking utensils and food. Your rucksack will need to be larger e.g. 50-80 litres, and camping could add 5-10 kg to its weight. Previous experience is advisable.

2·1 Heritage

Christian

From about the 7th century, Christianity began to make itself visible on remote moorlands with stone crosses. One of the most striking is Young Ralph, a tall slender cross about 7 miles offroute, adopted into its logo by the National Park. The Way passes another, albeit only its stump remains, namely Donna Cross: see page 34. There are many marker stones, some dating from the Bronze age, including the hand-stone and face-stone and Jenny Bradley: see page 36. The tradition grew up that travellers would leave coins, food or tokens at such stones. Myths also grew up about nocturnal gatherings and romances among the named stones.

In the Middle Ages, a hundred or so monastic foundations existed at one time or another in the North Riding of Yorkshire alone. Many orders of monks and nuns flourished, supported by large estates – often donated by nobles and successful merchants anxious to provide for their souls after death.

'Young Ralph'

Some of North Yorkshire's abbeys were of very ancient origin. The Way goes right past Whitby Abbey: see page 51. It passes very close to notable monastic foundations such as Rievaulx Abbey and Mount Grace Priory: see pages 25 and 31. Others such as Byland Abbey and Gisborough Priory are a few miles offroute. Details of the abbeys, priories and castles are on the English Heritage website: see page 61. Byland and Rievaulx were among the houses owned by the Cistercians, the order founded by Saint Bernard of Clairvaux who inspired the First Crusade. His followers played a significant part in improving agriculture in North Yorkshire.

The monasteries were all dissolved by Henry VIII after he broke with the Church of Rome. Many were given to his supporters, and the monks and nuns expelled. Most of the buildings were situated in remote rural areas and the new owners had little use for them. As a result, almost all are now ruins.

Maritime

Throughout its history, the coastal region has depended on the sea. Like most of the small coastal towns, Whitby has long been a fishing port and, having one of the best harbours, it was a flourishing centre for whaling boats for about 80 years in the late 18th and early 19th centuries. At its peak, in 1814, Whitby ships killed 172 whales, but the market for whale oil collapsed after gas replaced it as fuel for lamps. By 1830 only one whaling ship remained.

Whitby Abbey through the whalebone arch

Over time, fishing gave rise to a local shipbuilding industry. Local timber, mainly oak, was used to construct ocean-going ships. By the end of the 18th century, Whitby was the third largest shipbuilding town in England, after London and Newcastle. All three wooden ships in which Captain Cook (see page 39) undertook his voyages of Pacific exploration were built in the town's shipyards. The development of iron ships in the late 19th century and the growth of larger port facilities on the Tees led to the decline of shipbuilding in Whitby. The last wooden ship was launched in 1871 and the harbour then slowly silted up.

Industrial

Through much of its history, this area was fairly remote, with few towns of any size and an inhospitable coastline. There was little industry apart from North Yorkshire's virtual monopoly of the production of alum: see page 16. The Industrial Revolution was relatively late in arriving. Railways had reached towns such as Scarborough and Whitby by the 1840s, but their main impact was to encourage tourism. This was the time when the tradition of seaside holidays began to be established. The Grand Hotel at Scarborough symbolised the popularity of the area: see page 57.

The discovery of iron ore in the Cleveland Hills in the 1850s brought large scale industrialisation to the northern edge of the area: see page 17. Many mines were sunk, and massive quantities of ore were transported by rail to Middlesbrough for smelting. In 1830, it consisted of only a single farm, but by the end of the century the population had risen to almost 100,000. Middlesbrough had become the last new creation of the Industrial Revolution in Britain.

2·2 Geology and scenery

In the simplest terms, the geology lying underneath the Way can be described under three headings: Tabular Hills and valleys, North York Moors and North Sea coast.

The Tabular Hills, named after their tabletop shape, run from west of Helmsley almost all the way to the coast at Scarborough. They are mainly limestone, free-draining and fertile: they were formed about 150 million years ago when warm shallow seas covered this area, and you can think of them as fossilised coral reefs. Interspersed with limestone are layers of grit and, below that, a band of Oxford clay. The underlying rocks determine land use, with arable crops and grassland on the limestone and clay, and conifer plantations on the less fertile grits. The wide range of habitats encourages biodiversity: river valleys, pockets of dense woodland and forest, freshwater ponds, cliff face, farmland and rocky scrub. The Tabular Hills dominate the first two sections of the Way.

The central sections of the Way cross the North York Moors, at first following the spine of the Cleveland Hills. The high moors consist of sandstone rocks that erode slowly and form thin acid soils, lacking in nutrients. They are largely impermeable to water so drainage is poor and sphagnum moss bogs are common. Decomposition is slow and dead material builds up, eventually forming beds of peat. Thick layers of peat and other matter cause the bogs to dry out, encouraging heather, grasses and bilberry.

Approaching and along the coastal sections of the Way, from near Saltburn all the way to Filey, the underlying geology is mainly alluvium and glacial drift. Farm fields reach the very edge of the sea cliffs, and the beach and shore below change constantly with the tides. Coastal erosion is a persistent worry to those whose farmland and buildings are undermined by the relentless effects of weather and waves.

Overleaf, we describe the three main sources of mineral wealth from the Cleveland area: jet, alum and iron ore.

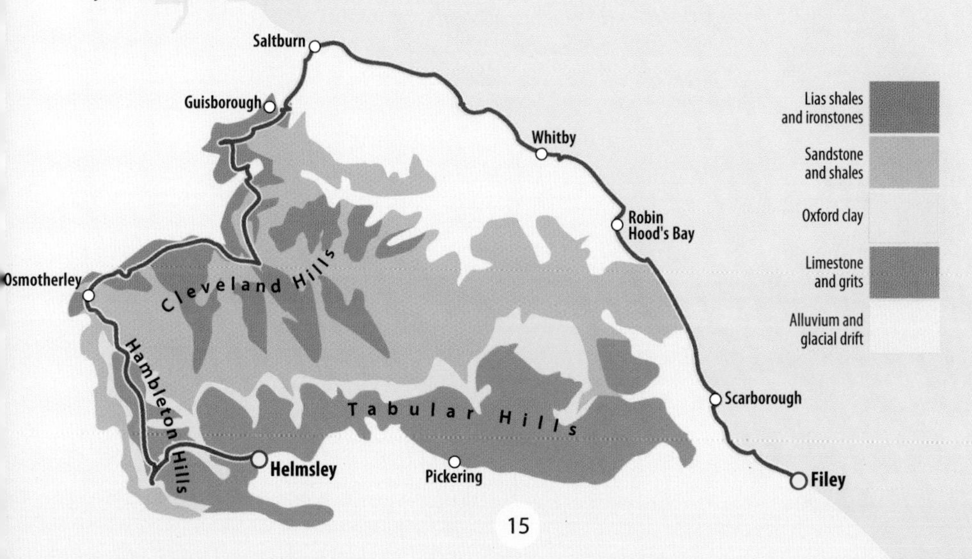

Jet

Jet (lignite) is a very hard rock that has been mined in the Cleveland area for 5000 years. It lends itself well to intricate carving and polishes to a high gloss. Carved jet ornaments have been found in Bronze Age barrows, but it wasn't until the 1800s that it began to be exploited commercially. The breakthrough was when lathes could first be used to polish the jet, thus making the most of its decorative potential.

A huge impetus was given by Queen Victoria's choice of mourning jewellery after the death of Prince Albert in 1861. Jet became popular and fashionable, with demand so high that by 1870 some 1400 men and boys were earning more than double the average wage in its extraction. Commercial mining took place all around the escarpment wherever the jet shales outcropped, but it was Whitby where jet was most celebrated. You can still find jet ornaments on sale in Whitby shops.

Alum

Alum (aluminium sulphate) was most valued for its ability to fix dyes, so that woollen garments would remain colour-fast after washing. It was also used in medicines and tanning. Its extraction in Yorkshire dates from about 1600, starting near Guisborough and spreading west along the hills and east to the cliffs. The industry thrived from about 1600 until 1871 when the works at Kettleness and Boulby closed.

Millions of tons of alum-bearing shale were quarried, changing the scenery permanently, especially near the coastline. (Shale is a fine-grained sedimentary rock composed of mud, clay and minerals.) The legacy of the alum working is obvious to the walker along long stretches of the Way, especially from Saltburn to Staithes and from Kettleness to Sandsend. It has left its mark on the weird snout of Kettle Ness and the collapsed sections of cliff and undercliff. Huge workings have left large areas barren: over 150 years later, even gorse has yet to establish a toehold. You may notice massive shale heaps and scars on the coastline at places such as Boulby, Kettleness and Sandsend.

Legacy of alum workings, Kettle Ness

The extraction process had many stages and must have created foul smells. After quarrying, the broken shale was mixed with wood, and later coal, for prolonged burning, often for months on end. Burned shale was then soaked in huge tanks of water with rotting seaweed and human urine. After boiling, crystallising and purifying, usable alum was finally extracted, at the price of appalling smoke, stench and heavy labour with pick and shovel. It took 50 to 100 tons of shale to create a single ton of alum. When simpler, cheaper dyeing methods were found in the mid-1850s, the alum industry declined abruptly, probably little lamented.

Iron ore

Ironstone was known to Britons in pre-Roman times, and the Rievaulx Estate was producing a ton a day of pig iron in the late 16th century. But large-scale iron mining began only in 1856, centred on Rosedale. At first the heavy, valuable ore had to follow a tortuous journey by rough tracks and roads. This led to the opening in 1861 of the Rosedale ironstone railway, a 20-mile stretch of standard-gauge railway over desolate moorland. Despite winter storms and blizzards, a total of over 10 million tons were transported on this line before its closure in 1929. The Way follows a short section of its trackbed on the approach to Bloworth Crossing: see page 36, bullet 4.

Peak production was reached in 1873 when half a million tons of iron ore were processed. Iron has to be extracted from the ore and purified, and also heated and oxidised in a process known as smelting. In order to make it harder and more malleable, controlled amounts of carbon are added to create steel or cast iron. This required lots of coal, coke and huge furnaces, and Durham and Middlesbrough grew massively on the strength of the iron industry. Some 370 million tons of Cleveland ore went to Teesside in the hundred years from 1860. By 1914, Cleveland mining had begun to decline and the last pit at North Skelton closed in 1964. The seams were not exhausted, indeed a vast quantity of ore is still buried deep under the moors, but they had become uneconomic. Nowadays, foreign ore is imported by sea at a fraction of the cost.

2·3 Habitats and wildlife

Roe deer doe

The wildlife along the Way reflects the underlying geology identified on page 15. We describe some of the species you are likely to see under the same three headings. The best times to spot wildlife are early morning and late evening; make the most of your chances by walking quietly and carrying binoculars.

Tabular Hills and valleys

The first part of the Way climbs up the escarpment of the Tabular Hills and heads north along the Hambleton Hills, through patches of farmland and woodland. These support many species of birds, especially tits (blue, great, coal and long-tailed) and woodpeckers. The woodland floor is home to wildflowers including primrose, violet, wood anemone and bluebells. The mammals you are most likely to see are brown hare or roe deer.

The walk through Nettle Dale takes you past large freshwater ponds, probably constructed by monks from Rievaulx for farming fish. Here you will see many kinds of ducks, most commonly mallard and tufted, and also perhaps moorhen and grey heron.

The limestone bedrock of these hills makes for good arable land, and where pastures are 'unimproved' you will see wonderful displays of lime-loving wildflowers in season: cowslip, dogwood, violet, marjoram, fairy flax and agrimony. Limestone grassland supports a wide variety of butterflies, including the common blue.

Wren

Common blue butterfly (male)

At Sutton Bank, visit the National Park Centre – about 80% of the Way lies within the National Park: see panel. Afterwards, you head north along the Hambletons with wonderful views and varied wildlife. Bird life ranges from the tiny russet-coloured wren darting among bushes and trees to the large birds of prey, including kestrel and buzzard, soaring overhead.

North York Moors National Park

This National Park celebrated its 60th anniversary in 2012. It is rich in history and pre-history with many religious monuments including the cross known as Young Ralph (see page 13), which it adopted in its logo. Its habitats include vast stretches of heather moorland, broadleaved woodlands, coastal cliffs, rivers and farmland. The park's resident population is about 25,000 heavily outnumbered by visitors, about 9 million pa, much less than most of England's National Parks. Its main Visitor Centre is near Danby, but the one at Sutton Bank lies on the Way and is open daily Feb to Oct, weekends only Nov to Dec; tel 01845 597426 **www.northyorkmoors.org.uk.**

North York Moors

The middle sections of the Way pass over the North York Moors – high heather moorland that at first follows the line of Cleveland Hills. This is the largest continuous expanse of heather moorland in England & Wales, and it is protected as home to internationally important numbers of breeding birds including merlin and golden plover. You'll see three kinds of heather: first to flower in July is bell heather with purple pink blooms, then the pale pink cross-leaved heath and finally the commonest, ling heather whose tiny pale pink flowers appear in mid to late August. Between them, they make an ocean of colour for several months of summer.

Sheep are everywhere, but they have to be hardy to survive the moorland climate – breeds such as the curly-horned Swaledale and long-coated Blackfaced. Their grazing creates gaps that allow other plants to thrive, and in places bilberry and cotton grass succeed in competing with the pervasive heather.

Swaledale sheep (ram)

Bell heather

Red grouse

The moors are managed for the game shooting of red grouse, whose raucous 'ge-back, ge-back' cry you will hear from afar. Red grouse feed on the new green shoots, but they need the taller heather for shelter and nest-building. So the landowners operate a system of controlled burning of patches of old heather in rotation, so as to encourage new young shoots while leaving plenty of older heather intact. Land managers also wage a constant war on the invasive bracken which occupies 20% of the National Park area.

In addition to red grouse, look out for three waders that arrive on the moorland in spring to breed: lapwing, curlew and golden plover. Lapwing are black and white with a rounded wing shape and an exuberant, wavering flight pattern; their 'peewit' call is distinctive. The curlew is Europe's largest wader, with a long down-curved beak and a strange cry like an old-fashioned whistling kettle.

Curlew

Golden plover

The golden plover also has a shrill, persistent call and amazingly effective camouflage – gold/black in summer and buff/white in winter – so its plumage blends into the moorland year-round. If you are alert, you may even spot the dashing, twisting flight of the merlin, Britain's smallest bird of prey, which makes its nest amongst banks of thick heather.

North Sea coast

From the clifftop path, there are continual great chances to view seabirds, especially in spring when they nest and breed in the crevices and narrow ledges, in some places (such as Whitby foghorn) forming closely packed colonies. Many kinds of gulls will make their piercing cries heard – herring, black-headed and great black-backed. The kittiwake is a medium-sized grey-backed gull which shows its black wing-tips in flight, and has short black legs.

The fulmar looks gull-like, but is actually a miniature cousin of the albatross, a stiff-winged master of updraughts, gliding and banking with shallow wingbeats. If one flies close to you, look closely at its hooked beak with tubular nostrils: like the albatross, it has special glands to dispose of excess salt.

Fulmar

Bar-tailed godwits at Skinningrove

Hardy vegetation clings to the cliff edges, often shaped into wild forms by the strong winds. Gorse, hawthorn and blackthorn bushes play host to small birds which, protected by their thorns, can rest, feed and shelter from predators. At any time of year you may see finches (seed eaters with characteristic heavy tapering bills) such as the chaffinch and the linnet, once popular as a caged songbird. Linnet numbers have dropped by 60% over the last 40 years, yet they are common hereabouts if you know where to look.

Linnet (male)

The Way descends to beach level from time to time, giving a closer view of other birds including shore waders: the handsome oystercatcher has smart black and white plumage, pink legs and a strong orange bill with which to probe for cockles and mussels. (You may also see them inland where they mainly feed on worms.) Other waders are seen at certain seasons only: for example, the bar-tailed godwit overwinters here but heads to the Arctic to breed. Its long straight bill is distinctive.

The North Sea is also rich in marine mammals, and you may well spot seals near the coastline, especially at low tide when they bask on rocks. Two kinds are found on this coastline: grey and common. Grey seals are larger and have more pointed heads, with dark brownish-grey fur. Common seals have a mottled coat and look more slender than greys, often arching their backs when ashore. If you carry binoculars, look at the nose: the common seal's nostrils make a pronounced V-shape.

Common seal

Helmsley

Market Square, Helmsley

The Way begins at the historic market town of Helmsley. It has become a centre for tourism in the Ryedale district, with traffic flowing through the town to the North York Moors, to the east coast, and to nearby attractions such as Rievaulx Abbey, Nunnington Hall, Castle Howard and Flamingoland. The pretty Borough Beck runs through the town from the moors to join the river at Rye Bridge: see photo below.

A traditional outdoor street market is held every Friday in the Market Square, which has several old coaching inns, an ancient market cross and an ornate Victorian monument to the second Baron Feversham. The Market Square has also become a popular weekend meeting place for motorcyclists, many of whom arrive via the scenic B-road from Stokesley, a favourite with local bikers. The North York Moors National Park has its headquarters in Bondgate nearby. All Saints Church has a lych-gate entrance and contains a collection of murals depicting the history of the church and the parish.

Overlooking the town are the ruins of Helmsley's Norman castle, managed by English Heritage (open daily April-September, weekends only out of season: see page 61). Behind the castle are the extensive grounds of Duncombe Park. The mansion house dates back to the 1750s, and its original five-acre walled garden has been restored in recent years, making a popular visitor attraction.

Helmsley Arts Centre runs a year-round programme of films, live music, talks, theatre performances, comedy and workshops. Helmsley no longer has any rail service, but there are bus links to stations at Malton, York and Scarborough.

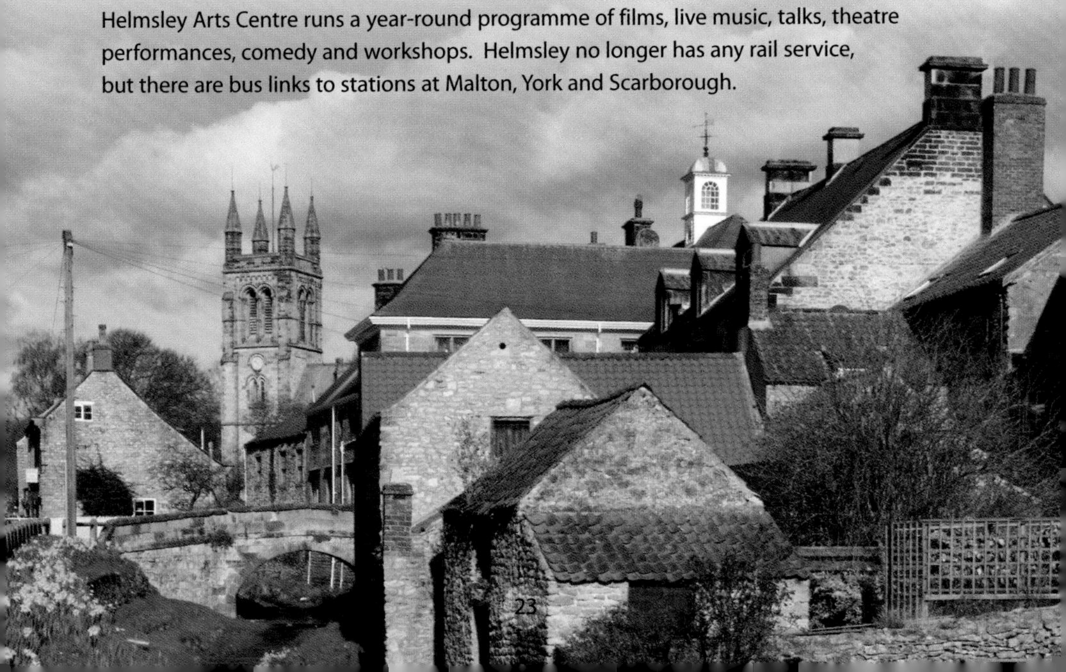

3·1 Helmsley to Sutton Bank

Map	**panel 1**
Distance	**10 miles (16 km)**
Terrain	**mixture of minor roads, good tracks and field paths which can be muddy in places**
Grade	**noticeable gradients, with more ups than downs**
Food and drink	**Helmsley (wide range), Hambleton Inn, National Park Visitor Centre**
Side-trips	**Rievaulx Abbey, National Park Visitor Centre**
Summary	**inspiring start through woods and rural villages to reach a wonderful elevated viewpoint**

Helmsley — 5½ / 9 — **Cold Kirby** — 3 / 5 — **White Horse** — 1½ / 2½ — **Sutton Bank**

- The Cleveland Way starts at the old Market Cross at the centre of Helmsley. Leave the Market Square by its north-west corner, and walk past All Saint's Church on the B1257 Stokesley Road.
- After 100 m, turn left up a street called Cleveland Way signed to Rievaulx. Pass a stone seat inscribed with placenames along the Cleveland Way, and go straight ahead (west) on the rising path. Eventually you'll see a similar seat at the end of the Way near Filey Brigg. As you climb the slope, the view behind is dominated by Helmsley Castle.
- In half a mile the path makes a dogleg, briefly left then right to follow the boundary wall beside mixed woodland. After a further half-mile go into the woods, and cross a small steep valley – Blackdale Howl. The stone steps here may be slippery.

East over Helmsley, with castle prominent

Griff Lodge

- The Way rises gradually and in almost half a mile passes Griff Lodge at an opening with views over the Rye valley. Continue ahead along the edge of Whinny Bank Wood, following the path as it descends to meet the road from Helmsley to Scawton.
- Turn left downhill beside the fence, until the bend is passed, with 1 mile of road walking ahead. Go west along the road towards the River Rye bridge.
- To visit Rievaulx Abbey, divert along the road that goes off right just before the bridge: see panel.

Rievaulx Abbey

Rievaulx was one of the first, most successful Cistercian abbeys to be founded in England, in 1132. Its name combines that of the Rye valley with the medieval French for valley 'vaulx'. The monks and lay brothers lived a self-sufficient life tending sheep on nearby moors, and trading wool and cloth with foreign merchants. Decline came in the 14th century with animal disease, and the population slumped after the Black Death circa 1350. Henry VIII dissolved the monasteries in 1538. The ruins are cared for by English Heritage and open daily April to September, weekends only out of season.

Cold Kirby

- After crossing the bridge, ignore a junction to the right signed 'Cold Kirby & Old Byland', and keep ahead until you reach a car parking area at a left bend.
- The Way leaves the road on a broad track off right, along Nettle Dale. Pass several large ponds, and at the fingerpost go over a feeder stream on stepping-stones. Continue along the forestry track ¾ mile to a Y-junction, and bear left beside a plantation in Flassen Dale.
- After about 300 m, follow the fingerpost to turn right out of the valley up a side gully. Bear left at a stile by a gate halfway up, on an improving surface. At a farm silo ahead, the track broadens and rises directly towards Cold Kirby along Low Field Lane.
- When the church tower comes into view, follow a path down to the right and into the village. Bear right up the main road with a line of sycamores on its left side.
- At the last house on the left (Cleveland Lodge), the Way is signed left along a green track (Cote Moor Road).
- The track makes a long gentle climb, then turns left and leads down to the edge of a forestry plantation. Here the Way turns right to pass a livery farm with gallops. At the fingerpost on the driveway to Hambleton House, turn left along it. Traffic noise heralds the busy A170 ahead.

Glider above Sutton Bank

- Turn right along the road verge past the Hambleton Inn and Casten Cottage, and cross at the Yorkshire Gliding Club road junction and sign. The Way now follows an earthwork (Casten Dyke) at an angle between the two roads, along a forest firebreak. At the end is a T-junction on the edge of the Hambleton Hills.
- The Way will shortly turn north from here to follow the edge of the escarpment, but first it diverts south (left) for one mile along the edge of Roulston Scar, past the gliding club, to visit the White Horse of Kilburn: see panel.
- Retrace your steps from the White Horse to the same T-junction. Now head north along the escarpment edge to reach the busy A170.
- Cross the road with care to twin timber posts. For the Sutton Bank National Park Centre (café, toilets and information) go ahead through the car park and picnic area. To continue the Way, instead turn left (west) along the path to a fingerpost with acorn, signed Sneck Yate.

White Horse of Kilburn

This hill figure is cut into the limestone of Roulston Scar on the edge of the tabular hills. It measures about 96 m by 69 m and covers 6500 square m (1.6 acres). Dating from 1857, it is said to have been created by a Kilburn schoolmaster, Thomas Hodgson, and his pupils.

The inspiration was a visit by local merchant Thomas Taylor to the bronze-age Uffington White Horse on the Berkshire Downs. Best viewed at a distance, the landmark can be seen from afar, such as from the tower of York Minster.

The White Horse of Kilburn

3·2 Sutton Bank to Osmotherley

Map	**panel 1**
Distance	**11½ miles (18½ km)**
Terrain	**mostly good paths, with some loose surfaces on moorland tracks; can be muddy near the end**
Grade	**mostly fairly easy with moderate gradients**
Food and drink	**National Park Visitor Centre, Osmotherley (shop, pubs and cafés)**
Summary	**easy level start with panoramic views, then over the moors along the drove road**

Sutton Bank — 3½ (5½) — Sneck Yate — 6 (9½) — Square Corner — 2 (3) — Osmotherley

- The Way heads north-west along the escarpment from the A170 along Sutton Brow, veering north after half a mile or so along the top of Whitestone Cliff.
- The route keeps fairly level and following the clear path is easy. A magnificent panorama opens up over Hood Hill, Gormire Lake and west to the distant Pennines – some say it's the best view in all Yorkshire. On a clear day, you can even see Great Whernside some 32 miles (51 km) away.
- After a sharp right turn the path bends around a great bowl, with South Woods below on your left and the grassland of Hambleton Down above on your right. At the highest point, where the path leaves the bowl, a grassy mound is all that remains of the Iron Age hill fort.

South-west over Gormire Lake

- After 2½ miles an enclosed section protects the path above a quarry, followed by a grassy path past High Barn. Soon the Way bears left slightly downhill to a gate into the plantation, to cross the Sneck Yate road, signed 'Forestry Commission, Boltby Forest'.
- Enter the forest on a sloping path, to emerge into a large field with scattered trees. Half a mile after Sneck Yate road you reach a farm road.
- Follow the right sweep of the road uphill to the farm at High Paradise. Do not turn left along the forest ride which you pass as you climb the hill. After the farm, the Way reaches Hambleton drove road at a junction: see panel.
- Turn left along the open section of the drove road, leading back into the forest. Where the ground is badly rutted, keep ahead on a narrow path on the right.

Hambleton drove road

This part of the Way is a historic route along which Scottish cattle were driven on foot to English markets in the 18th and 19th centuries. However, the road itself is much older. A rare Stone Age long barrow (burial mound) lies near the road and much archaeology has been discovered along the route. References in ancient documents such as the Rievaulx Cartulary confirm that the track (Hambleton Street) was used long before the Romans arrived and was one of the oldest roads in England. Look out for Steeple Cross beside the track – the remains of a medieval waymarker.

- You will emerge from the forest 1 mile beyond High Paradise farm at Steeple Cross; a rather inconspicuous standing stone is just right of the path after the gate.
- The path across Little Moor keeps close company with the boundary wall for the next 2 miles. At a boundary gate and cattle grid, bear left as the track sweeps around the shoulder of Black Hambleton.

The Way above South Woods

Paved path beyond Square Corner

- Soon the track descends past Hambleton End, with forestry on the left side. After a further 2 miles it meets the bend of a tarmac road at Square Corner. A sign 'Osmotherley 2 miles' leads the paved Way to the left from the road through bracken and heather.
- Descend steeply and skirt Oakdale Upper Reservoir on its right side. Keep left of the house, and go over a bridge near the Lower Reservoir. Don't follow the track down to the reservoir, but keep to the fenced track north-west and uphill.
- Cross the minor road, making a dogleg left for 40 m, then right along a track signed 'Osmotherley 1 mile'. Go up the track over the brow, and turn left through a narrow sheep sneck by the gates of White House Farm.
- Follow the diversion down to the right of the house and cross a footbridge over Cod Beck. Climb steeply from the valley, and cross fields along an enclosed path, to reach Osmotherley at Back Lane. Go straight ahead through the private-looking passageway into the main street.

Sheep sneck, Osmotherley

3·3 Osmotherley to Clay Bank

Map	panels 1 and 2
Distance	11 miles (17½ km)
Terrain	at first through farmland which can be muddy, then mostly on well-made paths
Grade	fairly easy at first, then a succession of steep ascents and descents
Food and drink	Osmotherley, Lord Stones café
Side-trips	Lady Chapel, Mount Grace Priory
Summary	a strenuous section over the switchbacks of the Cleveland Hills, with great views

Osmotherley		Huthwaite Green		Lord Stones		Clay Bank
	4½ miles / 7 km		3 miles / 5 km		3½ miles / 5½ km	

- Walk up North End past the Village Store and ignore a footpath sign on the left. After ¼ mile at the brow of the hill, the Cleveland Way turns left along Ruebury Lane.
- Follow the lane between houses as it bends around Ruebury Hill. The view opens up on the left hand side and the drone of traffic on the A19 may be heard.
- Two side-trips are options here: a footpath on the right leads within 400 m to Lady Chapel. And 300 m later on the left, there's a path via Chapel Wood Farm to Mount Grace Priory, ¾ mile off-route downhill.

Mount Grace Priory

This priory was founded in 1398 and is England's best preserved Charterhouse. Unlike most monks who took meals and worshipped together, Carthusians lived as hermits, even having meals passed into their cells. The reconstructed Cell 8 lets you see the austere furnishings and separate garden. You enter through the Lascelles Manor House (1654), rebuilt in about 1900 as an Arts & Crafts country house by Sir Lowthian Bell, a rich industrialist. It's cared for by English Heritage, open Thursday to Monday 10.00-18.00 in summer; weekends only out of season. Small admission charge, tel 01609 883494.

Mount Grace Priory

- The Way continues ahead and enters fields by a kissing-gate. Keep at first to the lower edge. After a mile, at a gate with clear signage you will meet the *Coast to Coast* footpath. The two routes converge and bear right up an inclined path traversing the hillside through woodland.
- The gradient eases on Beacon Hill as you pass the transmitter station. A little further on over the drystone wall, you may see the trig pillar – at 299 m (980 ft) this is the start of the Lyke Wake Walk (LWW): see panel.
- Over the hilltop, as the path begins to descend, the Way leaves the forest by a gate onto Scarth Wood Moor. Take the obvious signed path diagonally across, heading east.
- Where the path again converges with the boundary wall, and at a stone marked LWW, bear left down to the road crossing at Scarth Nick.

Lyke Wake Walk

This legendary challenge walk involves a 67 km (42 mi) crossing of the North York Moors. The walk starts at the Lyke Wake Stone and finishes about 2 km inland from Ravenscar on the coast, running parallel to Wainwright's Coast to Coast route for 26 km (16 mi).

According to the Lyke Wake Dirge, sung at 17th century Yorkshire funerals, everyone must traverse a wide, difficult moor after death. Those who have done good deeds will reach the end, others will go to hell. As originated by Bill Cowley, all who complete the route in under 24 hours may call themselves Dirgers of the Lyke Wake Club: see ***www.lykewake.org****.*

- Go left at the road for 50 m to a cattle grid, then right into the woodland. The path soon leads onto a forestry track and continues along level ground for about half a mile.
- At a viewpoint with two seats, another LWW stone marks a left turn. Beside the steep incline is a commemorative stone for Bill Cowley, creator of the LWW and author of an early Cleveland Way guidebook: see page 61.
- At the bottom of the incline go left and right across a path, turning south-east along the forest edge, with a farm and cottages visible across the valley.

East across Live Moor
(Roseberry Topping distant at left)

- After a further ¾ mile turn left across fields to a gate, then cross Piper Beck and Scugdale Beck over two fords, leading to the road in Huthwaite Green.
- Pass Hollin Hill Farm, and at the row of cottages cross the T-junction near a postbox, where a Cleveland Way sign points to 'Carlton Bank 2¾ miles'.
- The path rises behind bare slag heaps from old mine workings, and begins the steep climb of over 150 m (500 ft) vertical, through forest at first, then onto Live Moor. At last the gradient eases as you pass a large cairn on the plateau, and the way ahead is clearly visible towards Carlton Moor.
- After passing boundary stones along an easier half-mile section, the gradient again increases as the path nears the escarpment of Faceby Bank and Carlton Bank, climbing beside the glider runway to over 400 m elevation at Carlton Moor top. A trig pillar and boundary stone stand together at the summit.
- Within a few metres, the path begins its steep descent down to the 300 m contour at the road crossing (Raisdale Road). Take care on this and other downhill paths.
- Cross the road and look out for the Lord Stones café, which the Way passes: it's partly hidden by trees and built into a bank, bunker-style. Many a walker has fallen gratefully on its homemade food and fine choice of drinks.

South-west over Live Moor from Carlton Bank

Shelter at summit of Cringle Moor

- The Way continues east beside a fence at first, gradually becoming steeper as it climbs to the viewpoint on Cringle Moor, once more at 400 m altitude. The stone shelter includes a welcome seat, and faces a view indicator with memorial plaque to Alec Falconer: see page 61.
- Continuing along the escarpment, the Way climbs a little higher around Drake Howe before descending yet again to 300 m. The entrance tunnel and spoil heap of an old jet mine can be seen ahead as you cross the col. A boundary stone you pass in this section is known locally as Donna Cross.
- At a footpath sign to Gt Broughton, the Way doglegs to the right for 50 m before beginning the climb to 400 m – the highest point of Cold Moor. The path descends once more to 300 m across Garfit Gap before its final ascent to Hasty Bank and the Wain Stones.
- Several routes wind through the jumbled stones, some more of a scramble than others, but all paths join at the top. A further ¾ mile of path extends along the escarpment at almost 400 m before the final descent to the B1257 road at Clay Bank, the end of this strenuous section.

Approaching Cold Moor

North-east from the Wain Stones

3·4 Clay Bank to Kildale

Map	panel 2
Distance	9½ miles (15½ km)
Terrain	mostly well-made paths at first, then 2 miles (3 km) on minor roads
Grade	steep climb at first, then steady ascent to summit of the whole route at 454 m/1490 ft, remainder mainly descent
Food and drink	Kildale: Glebe Cottage tearooms (closed by 16.30 and all day Thursday)
Summary	an exposed crossing over high moors, then down to a sheltered rural village

Clay Bank — 3¼ / 5¼ — Bloworth Crossing — 6¼ / 10 — Kildale

- Cross the B1257 road and begin the steady climb to the highest point of the North York Moors at Round Hill. A sign points to Bloworth Crossing, which is 3¼ miles away.
- The path is steep for the first half mile until you reach the third gate, where the gradient eases on Carr Ridge. The path heads south-east, with boundary stones at intervals, mostly on the left of the path.

North-west from Carr Ridge over Hasty Bank

Bloworth Crossing

- Near the top of the climb, and 2 miles from Clay Bank, a track rises to join your path from the right. You'll see the unimpressive summit of Round Hill on the left.
- Take a path through the heather to the trig pillar marking the highest point of the Way (454 m/1490 ft). The boundary stone near the pillar is known as the hand-stone, and 200 m after returning to the path you will pass the aptly named face-stone.
- Ignore a track to the right after half a mile. The Way ahead begins to slope downhill, and bears off right on a narrow path at a left bend in the main track 1 mile after Round Hill.
- The narrow path crosses a damp area and rises to join the dismantled rail trackbed. Keep straight ahead (east) to reach Bloworth Crossing.
- Turn sharp left at Bloworth, slightly uphill. After half a mile you pass two distinctive standing stones – a tall boundary stone inscribed 1838, and the medieval shaft of a moors cross known as Jenny Bradley.
- Soon you pass a line of grouse butts on the left, then a Bronze Age burial site (Burton Howe) on the right. There's a fine view here, with Roseberry Topping prominent ahead.

Boundary stone and Jenny Bradley

Approaching Tidy Brown Hill

- Below Burton Howe, an interesting inscribed stone stands in the heather on the right of the track. It bears a roughly carved direction hand, and is dated 1757. Its inscriptions are easier to decipher than the previous hand-stone: *Stoxley* for Stokesley, *Gisbro* for Guisborough and *Kirby and Hemsley* for Kirkbymoorside and Helmsley.
- Nearly 2½ miles from Bloworth at Tidy Brown Hill, the Way forks right off the main track. A gate prevents vehicles from using the bridleway onto Battersby Moor.
- As you cross the moor, you may see Captain Cook's Monument ahead (see page 38) with Roseberry Topping to its left. Descend from Battersby Moor through two gates and go straight ahead on the tarmac road that joins you from the right.
- After half a mile, the road turns left across a cattle grid and descends towards Kildale. Below Park Nab you may spot rock climbers in action. The road starts to level out, and if staying at Kildale camping barn, follow the sign that takes you off left over a stile and down through a field to Park Farm. Otherwise, descend to the road junction and turn right to reach Kildale after 500 m.

Climbers on Park Nab

3·5 Kildale to Saltburn by the Sea

Map	**panels 2 and 3**
Distance	**14½ miles (23½ km)**
Terrain	**mostly well-made paths and tracks, a few muddy; some roads and pavements**
Grade	**generally undulating route with several testing gradients ending with long descent**
Food and drink	**Slapewath (pub), Skelton Green (pub), Skelton (shop, pubs, café), Saltburn**
Summary	**a long section of moors and forest with fine views, then across the busy A171 into pleasant farmland and a heritage trail, finally reaching the coast at Saltburn**

Kildale		Roseberry Topping		Slapewath		Saltburn
	4¼ / 7		6 / 9½		4¼ / 7	

- Go down the road into Kildale and at the fingerpost turn left towards the railway station. Within 50 m go right at Glebe Cottage Tearoom (in summer 2012 open 11.30-16.30). Follow the tarmac lane under a railway bridge and over the River Leven.
- The road winds up quite steeply past Bankside Cottage and Farm, with views opening up behind. Continue uphill on the road until you reach a car parking area at the brow. Turn left along the forestry track, signed 'Gribdale 2 miles'.
- After about 300 m, bear left off the main track onto a path through larch woodland. Emerging through a barrier, 2 miles after Kildale, you gain your first close view of Captain Cook's monument ahead, with Roseberry Topping, your next objective, now to its right. The last section to the obelisk at 324 m/1063 ft is stone-paved and steep.

Captain Cook (1728-1779)

James Cook was born in Cleveland and attended school in Great Ayton. He went to sea aged 18 and gained 10 years' experience on the east coast of England. In 1755 he joined the Royal Navy, soon qualifying as a master navigator. His three major Pacific voyages started in 1768. He was the first to chart distant coastlines accurately, including most of north-west America and the south Pacific. He made major advances in navigation and in preventing scurvy. In 1778 he discovered Hawaii, the scene of his gruesome death a year later.

Cook's monument, Roseberry Topping distant

- At the monument, bear right down the paving, north towards Roseberry Topping. Keep to the obvious wide path down into the valley, ignoring any apparent short-cuts on the left. After half a mile you reach Gribdale Gate car parking and picnic area.
- Make a dogleg to the right across the road and climb steps on the path signed 'Roseberry Topping 2 miles'. The Way continues onto Great Ayton Moor and keeps the splendid drystone boundary wall on its left for 1¼ miles.
- At the end of the forest, a gate in the corner of the stone wall leads onto the path to Roseberry Topping. Go through the gate for the 1¼ mile round trip to the summit at 320 m (1050 ft), steeply downhill at first, then uphill. The effort is rewarded by a superb 360° panorama, south to the Cleveland Hills, north and west to Teesside and north-east to the coast. Nearby to the south is Aireyholme Farm where James Cook lived from 1735, attending school in Great Ayton which lies to the south-west.
- Afterwards retrace your steps to the gate, and take the centre path (east). In ¼ mile bear right along the edge of a plantation. After a further half-mile at a junction turn right away from the trees for 100 m on a broad track.

Roseberry Topping

Approaching Highcliffe Farm

- At the sign, turn left (east) onto a narrow paved section, with Highcliffe Farm visible ahead. The Way converges with its boundary wall, and climbs past it to the edge of Guisborough Woods in under 1 mile.
- Follow signs carefully through Guisborough Woods. Go through the kissing-gate and along the path to bear up right in 100 m, away from the boundary wall. After 50 m cross a forest drive, and continue on a narrow path around the hill.
- To visit Guisborough and its priory, turn left down the forest drive: see page 43 for this major diversion, which rejoins the Way at Slapewath.
- Climb steeply up steps beside the crags to reach the top of Highcliff Nab. There are spectacular views north over Guisborough and north-east to the coast.
- Go along the edge of the escarpment to rejoin the drive you crossed earlier, now heading east. At the first track junction go straight ahead. At the second junction fork left downhill.

North-east from Highcliff Nab

- The track joins another forest drive at a lower level. Keep ahead, north-east, on an improved surface. Soon the Way strangely diverts onto a narrow path on the left of the main track for a short distance, only to rejoin it at the top of a rise.
- At a wide junction of forest tracks, take the left fork. Keep ahead on the level track for a further half-mile and cross another track at a junction.
- Just after you approach a dilapidated estate wall, you start to see villages ahead in the distance. At a right bend of the track, the Way turns left, crossing the line of the wall. Proceed along the edge of forest, with an open field on the right.
- At the end of the field bear right to cross a gully, still following the forest edge. At a junction, turn left down a concrete drive. In 250 m where the surface changes to tarmac, turn sharp right onto a narrow path.
- The path broadens into mixed woodland with traffic noise increasing ahead. At an open area used by offroad motorbikes, keep close to the fence on the right. Follow signs carefully through a series of narrow gates along the level woodland path, watching out for motorbikes.
- At the end in half a mile, turn left down a wider track towards the busy A171 road. Go left along a tarmac path parallel with the road for 100 m and cross over by a bus shelter. Continue left along the opposite footway.
- Go past the Fox and Hounds, and at the road signed Slapewath turn right. At the far end of some white houses, turn uphill following the Cleveland Way sign 'Skelton Green 2 miles'. (Near the pub, ignore a sign for 'Cleveland Street Trail' – marked 'Skelton Green 1½ miles': this is not your route.)
- Behind the houses, climb steeply on a flight of steps around the right hand side of a large quarry. At a bench above the quarry, bear right (north) up the steepest path.
- At the top the path levels out and follows field boundaries, soon turning to the right. Continue for just over a mile past Airy Hill Farm down its access road, along Airy Hill Lane and into Skelton Green.
- After passing the back of the Green Inn, cross the main road and enter an enclosed path which leads over the hilltop and down towards Skelton. Keep ahead in front of bungalows for 30 m, and turn left down steps towards Skelton High Street.
- Cross over directly to a newsagent shop and go down Coniston Road. Take the first right turn into Derwent Road.

Enclosed path towards Skelton

- Follow Derwent Road downhill all the way to a fence across its bottom end, where a signed path leads north across open ground towards some more houses.
- Cross a road at the sign 'Saltburn 1 mile'. Go through the valley to an underpass (beneath the A174) and along a field path to enter the wooded gorge of Skelton Beck. Go all the way down the valley to cross it by a footbridge, then pass under the tall railway viaduct.
- The Way now follows part of the Marske Mill Heritage Trail. Turn left uphill at a junction, then turn right at an ornate metal seat, beside a sign Saltburn Valley Gardens.
- Continue along the main path ignoring turns to left and right, until you reach another sculptured oak-leaf bench. Turn left up the steep path to the road at the top.
- The Way continues right along Glenside to pass a children's play area, war memorial, and bandstand, but most walkers will divert left to the facilities of the town centre.
- Follow the road down to the sea front. You can shortcut the road bends behind the Spa Hotel on steps.

Railway viaduct over Skelton Beck

Diversion to Guisborough

- This diversion misses out 3½ miles of forest paths, and lets you visit the market town of Guisborough with its shops, services and priory ruins. Afterwards, a direct path from the priory along the Cleveland Street Trail rejoins the Way at Slapewath, at the cost of very little extra walking distance overall.
- From the forest drive (page 40 bullet 3) walk downhill and at the first junction turn right to stay on the main drive, soon ignoring an elaborate metal fingerpost for the Tees Link Path. Keep ahead on the main drive ignoring all minor paths to left and right.
- After 1 mile, at a main junction a branch path is signed 'Walkway Visitor Centre' to the left. Keep straight ahead, following instead the fingerpost 'Guisborough Market Town via Forest'. In a further ½ mile the signed track leads into Belmongate and directly to the town centre under an old railway bridge.
- At the end of Belmongate cross the junction into Bow Street and bear right into Church Street. You will arrive at the priory entrance before reaching St Nicholas Parish Church on the right. The Cleveland Street Trail begins to the left of the church along a narrow path where you pass through a metal kissing-gate.
- Cleveland Street takes a direct line across fields to reach Whitby Road near the main entrance gates of Gisborough Hall. Cross the road and continue along the Foxdale Farm access road with another fingerpost 'Cleveland Street' guiding the way.
- In 100 m leave the farm track at a bend and maintain direction following the 'Footpath' fingerpost. In ½ mile across fields you will converge with the busy A171 near Slapewath. Follow a short section of Cleveland Street in the valley bottom, then after 200 m take steps onto the roadside pavement. Walk east along the road past a scrapyard, and cross over at signs for Slapewath to rejoin the Way.

East over Gisborough Priory

3·6 Saltburn by the Sea to Sandsend

Map	**panels 3 and 4**
Distance	**17 miles (27½ km)**
Terrain	**mostly grass and field paths which can be muddy; some pavement, beach and shore**
Grade	**undulating route, with many steep gradients; highest point reached at Rock Cliff (over 200 m/650 ft)**
Food and drink	**Saltburn, Skinningrove, Staithes, Runswick, Sandsend (wide range)**
Summary	**a strenuous day along the coast with many points of historic interest; bracing sea views and imposing sea cliffs punctuated by hidden coves**

Saltburn		Skinningrove		Staithes		Runswick Bay		Sandsend
miles	4		5		3		5¼	
km	6½		8		5		8½	

Saltburn is an amazing place. Its thriving arts scene seems out of all proportion to its modest population (6000) with events such as art exhibitions, film and jazz nights, vintage fairs and beer and folk festivals. Old Saltburn was a tiny fishing village and smugglers' haven, transformed in 1861 into a Victorian seaside resort with handsome architecture including the railway viaduct, seaside pier and cliff lifts. The founder of modern Saltburn was Henry Pease – railway owner, philanthropist and Member of Parliament. While continuing to celebrate 150 years of its Victorian past, the town has reinvented itself for the 21st century with a lively leisure scene including health and wellbeing, restaurants and superb surfing.

Britain's oldest surviving water-balanced cliff lift

West over Saltburn

- Cross Skelton Beck and go past the beached boats and tractors nearby. Take the path up steps behind the Ship Inn, signed to Skinningrove 3½ miles. At the top, look behind you for great views over Saltburn, and Roseberry Topping briefly returns to view.
- Route finding is easy along the clifftop path. The entire coastline from Saltburn to Scalby Ness is recognised as the North Yorkshire and Cleveland Heritage coast. The Way goes through Hunt Cliff Nature Reserve, and in a little over 1 mile passes the site of a Roman signal station, with an information board.
- Soon the path is in close company with the railway line around the edge of Warsett Hill, and passes the Guibal Fanhouse and information board after 2 miles. The jetty at Skinningrove and the steelworks above the town can be seen ahead.
- From Cattersty Cliffs, follow the path down steps to the sands below. The Way reaches Skinningrove over low dunes and through a gap in the old jetty. Go past cottages (Marine Terrace) and over the Kilton Beck Bridge.

Guibal Fanhouse

- Leave the road at the sign and climb steps up the cliff edge again. In less than 1 mile pass above Hummersea beach and follow the CW signs soon to turn inland, bypassing a small farm. Pass to the right of a stable building where there's a stile.

Skinningrove Bay with jetty

- The path regains the cliff edge above extensive alum workings, reaching its highest point near Rockhole Hill (212 m/695 ft), identified by trig point and mast nearby. You are walking above Rock Cliff, the highest cliff anywhere on England's east coast.
- The Way overlooks the huge alum quarry workings for more than 1½ miles, returning to the cliff edge approaching cottages at Boulby. Go along the road past the row of cottages and keep straight on. At a bend in the road, with the grey chimneys of Boulby potash mine in view, continue straight ahead (east) onto a grassy path.
- Cross the field paths for half a mile to join the old coast road (Cowbar Lane) where cliff erosion has claimed part of it. A fence protects the Way from the edge, to rejoin the lane into Staithes.
- Go left down the road to the village and over the footbridge into the main street, to pass the Royal George. Go ahead past the Cod and Lobster, and turn right up Church Street. There's a plaque recording Cook's apprenticeship in Staithes on the right.
- At the top of Church Street continue ahead, signed to Port Mulgrave. Bear left at a fingerpost to pass by a farm. The Way follows two large field edges to rejoin the cliff at the top of a steep rise.
- Walk along the road to Port Mulgrave, and turn left at the fingerpost for Runswick Bay. Ignore a footpath to the left here. The Way keeps level along the road and around the jumble of Rosedale Cliffs, returning to the cliff edge as it makes its way towards Runswick.

- There are two small ravines to negotiate along the cliff path, before arriving at the road through the car park of the Runswick Bay Hotel. At the road, turn left to pass the Cliffemount Hotel, where a path winds down to the lower part of Runswick bank. (Alternatively you can cross over at the Runswick Bay Hotel and walk straight down the steep bank on the road.)

Boats moored at Staithes

- At a turning circle, keep on down towards the shore. In stormy weather, the next section may not be passable at high tide: if need be, wait for the sea to retreat a bit. Otherwise, continue across the sand for 500 m past the painted timber buildings of the sailing club, where a green sign points to the Cleveland Way up the next gully.
- Go past the base of cliffs (with caves known locally as *hob-holes*) and find the narrow gully entrance. A handrail offers some help along the slippery shale. Go forward 20 m, cross the stream and climb steeply up the long flight of steps.

Staithes

The Way crossing a ravine near Runswick

- Resume the grassy clifftop path after the steep climb, soon passing an old railway embankment on your right.
- A further ¾ mile along the cliffs, turn left in front of the farm at Kettleness: don't miss the sign on this telegraph pole. Sandsend is now just over 3 miles ahead.
- After the farm road a fingerpost sends you left to rejoin the cliff path, and the Way sweeps around two fields to meet the dismantled rail track. Walk a few metres to the right of the path to see the old tunnel entrance in the cutting.
- Go along the field edge cliff path for another mile, ignoring a right turn signed Lythe. Very soon the Way bends to the right side field boundary, away from the edge, and directly towards a gap in the fence, into woodland. Climb carefully down the steep steps into the workings of the former Sandsend alum quarries.
- Look back to see the other end of the rail tunnel. The Way joins the railway trackbed for the remaining mile to Sandsend.

Runswick Bay

3·7 Sandsend to Robin Hood's Bay

Map	panel 4
Distance	10 miles (16 km)
Terrain	sandy beach or tarmac roads to Whitby, then grassy cliff paths, sometimes muddy
Grade	a few steep gradients, but mostly fairly easy
Food and drink	Sandsend, Whitby, Robin Hood's Bay (wide range)
Side-trip	Whitby Abbey
Summary	the long sandy strand leads to busy Whitby, then the clifftop path passes above smugglers' coves and dramatic headlands, ending at Robin Hood's Bay

Sandsend — 3 / 5 — Whitby — 4 / 6½ — Maw Wyke Hole — 3 / 5 — Robin Hood's Bay

- If the tide is out, you could walk all the way from Sandsend to Whitby along the beach, a distance of just over 2½ miles from slipway to slipway.
- Alternatively, cross the bridge over Sandsend Beck and follow the A174 road past the Beach Hotel. Go over another bridge at East Row and pass the Hart Inn. Continue along the road as it veers away from the shore.

Sandsend

- Go along the road as it climbs beside Whitby golf club, and take the left turn down into a ravine. The path goes under a golfers' footbridge, presenting a choice of routes; upper or lower.
- The official Way climbs up the tarmac path to the cliff top and stays beside the road leading into Whitby at high level. Alternatively, especially in fair weather and at any state of tide, continue down the ravine and use the concrete road along the sea defences until the North Beach café/bar below the Metropole Hotel, near the Spa Whitby Pavilion Complex.
- If you choose the lower route, there are several paths near the Spa that lead up to the higher level on an easy gradient. Either way you will arrive at an impressive statue of Captain Cook overlooking Whitby harbour.
- Cross the road and take the steps down beneath a whalebone arch. The Khyber Pass road snakes down to the quayside bandstand. Go right towards the swing bridge, between amusement arcades and the fish market.
- Cross the River Esk over the swing bridge, and turn left into Sandgate. Go right in the small Market square past the Town Hall, and turn left along Church Street. This in turn leads into Henrietta Street, and to the Church Stairs.
- Now climb the 199 steps leading to St Mary's Church and Whitby Abbey. In the graveyard of St Mary's is Caedmon's Cross, a tribute to the earliest English poet whose name we know.
- Go around the abbey perimeter and look for the left turn sign to the cliff top. From here it's a further 6½ miles (10.5 km) to Robin Hood's Bay.

Statue of James Cook

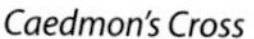

Caedmon's Cross

Whitby

This seaside town has a rich and varied heritage – maritime, ecclesiastical and mineral. From his plinth on Whitby's west cliff, the statue of Captain Cook overlooks the harbour: see pages 38 and 50. In 1768, the 40-year old James Cook left here as commander of the Whitby-built *HM Bark Endeavour* on the first of his three voyages of exploration and charting. Whitby soon became England's third largest ship-building town, as well as a major whaling port.

The ruins of Whitby Abbey (see side-panel) dominate the town from its east cliff, and are an important landmark in early Christianity. It was here that the crucial Synod of Whitby decided in AD 664 to interpret Christianity according to the Roman, rather than the Celtic, version.

Today, Whitby has the atmosphere of a quirky English seaside town. In season, it is thronged with tourists and its curious range of shops speak of its history – of colliers and cobles, shipwrecks and smuggling, jet-mining and Jurassic fossils. Whitby's literary tradition is also strong, most famously as the setting for Bram Stoker's gothic novel *Dracula.*

Whitby Abbey

An Anglo-Saxon monastery for men and women was founded here in AD 657, first ruled by a remarkable Saxon princess, St Hild. What stands today is the ruin of the early gothic abbey started in 1220 and suppressed by Henry VIII in the 16th century. Further damage was done by storms, erosion and shell damage during World War 1. The nearby Cholmley family mansion is home to an award-winning visitor centre with valuable finds from the site, and modern interactive experiences. The site is cared for by English Heritage and open daily April-October (weekends only out of season): *see page 61.*

Whitby Abbey

- After almost 1 mile along the cliff top, pass the static homes and caravans at Saltwick Bay. Keep straight ahead on the main road. The remaining 5 miles to Robin Hood's Bay is along clifftop paths.
- After 1 mile pass the Whitby Fog Signal Station, and go around the lighthouse perimeter wall. Nearly a further mile beyond, steps lead across two ravines.
- After another half-mile, at the next ravine of Maw Wyke Hole, the *Coast to Coast* route joins you for the last three miles into Robin Hood's Bay.
- Once you spot a white coastguard lookout building (slightly inland), look for the distant headland to its right – the South Cheek of Robin Hood's Bay.
- Nearly two miles after Maw Wyke Hole, pass below the lookout station to reach North Cheek (Bay Ness), cared for by the National Trust. After you round the headland, the village comes into view, and you pass a Rocket Post field: see panel.
- The path leads through a gate into Mount Pleasant North. At its end turn left into Station Road, and at the car park opposite the Victoria Hotel, bear right to descend steeply down New Road almost to the sea.

Rocket posts

This post is a replica of one used here from 1923 to 1980. Rocket posts were once common on this coastline, used as target practice by the coastguard, aiming at the post instead of a ship's mast. The rocket, attached to a light rope, was fired at the mast of a boat in distress. The rope was used to haul across a hawser (heavy rope), which carried a 'breeches buoy' – a lifebuoy with canvas shorts attached. Crew members stepped into the shorts to be winched, one by one, direct from the boat to safety. Rescue by rocket continued until it was superseded by the Sea King helicopter.

Towards North Cheek, with South Cheek just visible at right

Robin Hood's Bay

The long history of this area stretches back to the Bronze age, with evidence of burials nearby. Later, Roman, then Saxon and Norse settlements came and went. The origin of the name is unknown, but there is no evidence for any association with the legendary folk hero. Locally, the village is known simply as 'Bay'.

By the 18th century, its secluded location had made it Yorkshire's busiest smuggling port. To evade the excise collectors, local people built a maze of underground hiding places with passages linking the houses. Later, fishing became the mainstay of the village, with its heyday in the mid 19th century when about 170 ships were based there. A coastguard station was opened in 1822, and the first lifeboat launched in 1830.

Violent storms lashed the coast, and in 1836 the Bay Hotel was washed away (but rebuilt soon afterwards). It wasn't until the early 1950s that the present 12m-high sea wall was built. The village's growing popularity with visitors was boosted by the opening of the Whitby to Scarborough railway in 1885. This sadly was axed by Beeching in 1965 and today's visitors come by car, bus or in some cases on foot, following the Coast to Coast or Cleveland Way routes.

3·8 Robin Hood's Bay to Scarborough

Map	**panels 4 and 5**
Distance	**14½ miles (23½ km)**
Terrain	**mostly grassy paths and tracks, can be muddy and slippery after rain**
Grade	**moderate gradients with a steep climb to Ravenscar at 200 m/650 ft, following coastal contours all the way**
Food and drink	**Bay (wide range), Ravenscar (tearooms March/Oct), Scarborough (wide range)**
Summary	**a long section from dramatic sea cliffs to the east coast's most famous Victorian spa resort of Scarborough**

- Very near the bottom of New Road, look for Albion Road on the right. Turn here, and in 50 m go left up narrow stone steps. A wooden stairway continues the Way up to the right, and onto the undulating cliff path. Within the next mile this will return you twice down to beach level and back up again.
- Alternatively, at low tide only, you could instead take the wooden steps down to the beach and walk along it for ¾ mile to Boggle Hole, or 1 mile to Stoupe Beck Bridge.
- On the upper Cleveland Way route, look out for a left turn into an enclosed path between fences. The path soon leads to a tunnel cut through dense blackthorn, down steep steps to the Youth Hostel at Boggle Hole.
- Cross the footbridge where a sign points to Ravenscar 2½ miles. The Way regains the cliffs, but soon drops down again to cross Stoupe Beck. After the footbridge, climb steeply to Stoupe Bank Farm and turn left along the road.

View across Robin Hood's Bay to North Cheek

- After 250 m, beyond a dip, go left through a gap in the wall to rejoin the cliff path near a wartime bunker. The large building on the skyline ahead is Raven Hall, a historic hotel at Ravenscar, and your next goal. The route follows the cliff path for 1 mile, then turns inland.
- Follow signs carefully from the main track where the Way forks right steeply on a red shale path. As you approach Ravenscar, the surface of the paths becomes studded with bricks from the former brickworks.
- Pass the National Trust visitor centre and shop as you approach the gates of Raven Hall hotel. A CW sign points to Scarborough 11 miles. Go along Station Road and turn left in 100 m along an unsurfaced road leading to the cliff path.
- After about 500 m, a sign 'Tearooms' points off right to the former Ravenscar station and its square, with an information board and plan of 'the town that never was'.
- After visiting Ravenscar, return to the path and follow it through a field with a rocket post. Within 1 mile pass the old coastguard lookout station and wartime radar site.

Ravenscar

The poster above shows the high hopes held by the developers of creating a health resort to rival Whitby or Scarborough, but the deserted station square that you can visit from the Way tells the reality. The venture began in 1895 but by 1913 the company had gone bankrupt. Brickworks, alum quarries and railway are now long gone, and only the hotel, complete with golf course and swimming pool, remains. The views of Robin Hood's Bay from its hanging gardens are exceptional: see below.

North-west over Robin Hood's Bay from Raven Hall

Ravine near Cloughton Wyke

- The Way continues along the clifftop, with views ahead past Scarborough headland with castle prominent, all the way to the long low snout of Filey Brigg.
- About 3 miles after the radar site the path descends to cross Hayburn Beck at Hayburn Wyke: take care on the steep steps down into the valley.
- Cross the footbridge, turn right uphill and follow signs carefully as the Way continues on the far side, twisting left, then right. Beware: several paths run through the woods.
- Reach the next large inlet, Cloughton Wyke, after a further 1½ miles. Three small ravines punctuate the path around it. Soon climb steps up to the cliffs of Hundale Point, overlooking Hundale Scar.
- Shortly after the coastguard lookout post at Long Nab, the Way heads inland: cross a path leading to Burniston village in a dogleg, and stick to the clifftops for another 2 miles of easy walking to Scalby past Long Nab and Cromer Point.
- As you approach Scalby, pass a sign pointing inland 'Helmsley 48 miles' – the start of the Tabular Hills Walk: see page 61. Follow it if you are staying at the Youth Hostel (just over 1/2 mile away) or any of the campsites along Burniston Road (about 1/2 mile).
- Otherwise continue to Scalby Ness, the next headland, where the Way cuts the corner – but you may prefer to stick to the coastline to enjoy the superb views.
- Just half a mile further on you reach steps leading down to a footbridge over Scalby Beck at Scalby Mills, on Scarborough's north bay. Follow the north bay promenade past the white-roofed Sea Life Centre, towards the town.

South past Hayburn Wyke to Long Nab

Scarborough

Diving Belle sculpture beside lighthouse

From a great distance, the walker's view of Scarborough is dominated by the prominence of the castle headland with its tall keep. Since the first castle was built here in 1136, its history has been turbulent – capture, recapture, extension and siege, with bomb damage during World War 1.

Scarborough is England's top tourist destination on the east coast, having captured visitors since Victorian times with its combination of coastal scenery, spa waters (discovered in 1626) and easy access by railway from York (1845). The Grand Hotel, originally with 365 bedrooms, was Europe's largest at the time of its completion (1867).

The town today has a growing creative and digital economy, with attractions ranging from sandy beaches, Peasholm Park and cliff lifts to free wifi (seafront and harbour area) and the UK's largest Star Disk; the latter has subterranean lights showing the 42 brightest stars and constellations visible in the night sky.

The town is home to England's most successful living playwright, Sir Alan Ayckbourn. From 1972-2009 he was artistic director of the Stephen Joseph Theatre where nearly all his plays had their first performance. The superbly restored Spa Complex is home to many concerts, including those of Britain's only remaining seaside orchestra.

Although most of the town appears to be at a safe height above the North Sea, in 1993 a dramatic landslip took the large Holbeck Hall Hotel down the cliff and washed it into the sea. The Cleveland Way (which formerly ran above the Spa Complex) has been diverted to run at sea level ever since. Scarborough has two tourist information centres – at the harbour and in the town centre (Brunswick Centre).

Across south bay to Scarborough's sea front and castle

3·9 Scarborough to Filey Brigg

Map	**panel 5**
Distance	9½ miles (15½ km)
Terrain	**mostly grassy paths and tracks, can be muddy and slippery after rain**
Grade	**moderate gradients, following coastal contours**
Food and drink	**Scarborough (wide range), Filey (wide range)**
Summary	**an easy clifftop ramble to reach the end at Filey Brigg**

Scarborough 1½ — 2½ Spa Complex — 3½ — 5½ — Cayton Bay — 4½ — 7¼ — Filey Brigg

- There's a long walk along Scarborough's sea front: it's about 3 miles from the Sea Life Centre around the castle headland, past the harbour and to the Spa. We have simply halved this distance in our diagram above, but take advice about where best to leave the sea front for your accommodation. Most of the town sits high on the headland and access by road or cliff lift is limited.
- The Way passes the Spa Cliff Bridge, built in 1827, *en route* to the handsome Spa Complex. From here it's a further 8 miles to the end of the Way at Filey Brigg.
- Leave Scarborough's south bay uphill on a broad track visible ahead, signed 'Filey 8 miles'. Where the track bends up right to meet the road, leave it to continue ahead on a narrow gorse-lined path with great views behind you.
- Soon you arrive at the cliff edge and skirt around Wheatcroft Cliff golf course. The Way is well signed across a small wooded ravine, and after half a mile between field and woodland, the path approaches houses at Knipe Point.

Across south bay, with Spa Complex and Grand Hotel at left

North-west over Cayton Bay

- Because of coastal erosion, the Way has been permanently diverted inland here. Turn right beside the houses for 250 m, then it's left along Filey Road for 500 m. A fingerpost points you steeply down a stepped path into woodland. At a junction turn right, thus resuming the line of the former path.
- Soon the Way leads to an opening with the sandy beach of Cayton Bay in view. Follow signs along the undercliff, to a gate. The path now rises steeply beside a fence to the cliff top. Cayton Bay has the remains of several World War 2 pillbox lookouts: most have fallen to the beach below, but at the eastern end of the bay, a sole survivor teeters, clinging to the cliff edge.

WW2 pillbox above Cayton Bay

North-east over Filey Brigg

- Cross fields and a beach road below Cayton Bay Holiday Village. Head straight towards the edge of Lebberston Cliff, passing to the left of a cottage.
- The remaining three miles follow the undulating clifftop path to Filey Brigg. You pass several caravan sites close to the cliffs at Gristhorpe, and around a deep inlet – the Wyke.
- You start to see Filey town to your right and pass along the top of Newbiggin Cliff, leading to North Cliff and a white-painted restored rocket post in the field on your right.
- Two miles after the Wyke, you reach the official end of the Way at Filey Brigg, marked by a fingerpost 'Helmsley 109 miles'. Congratulations on completing the Cleveland Way!

Stone seat at Filey Brigg

The stone seat here, like the one at Helmsley, is inscribed with placenames from along the Cleveland Way – but only on its left side. Its right side carries placenames from the 79-mile Yorkshire Wolds Way, for which this is also the terminus. Could this be your next challenge?

From here, most people walk the final mile into the centre of Filey. Go south through the Country Park, passing public toilets and heading for St Oswalds Church. Metal fingerposts signed 'Town Centre' point you past the church to a footbridge over Church Ravine. Still heading south, follow Church Street to the roundabout and along Station Road to the next roundabout. The bus station is on your left, or turn right across the railway for the train station.

4 Reference

History of the Cleveland Way

The route has a long history: Alan Falconer (author of the first guidebook, see below) traces it back to a long walk along the moors and cliffs that his father made in 1913. However, the main impetus came in the 1930s, just after the Youth Hostels Association was formed. The idea of a recreational walk intended to link up Youth Hostels was then ahead of its time.

The National Parks Commission took up the idea in 1953, at first under the unwieldy title of the 'North York Moors and Yorkshire Coast Path'. Some 16 years later, in May 1969 the Cleveland Way was officially opened – fittingly at Helmsley Youth Hostel. It was one of Britain's earliest National Trails, second only to the Pennine Way (1965). Many would rate it more highly because of its greater variety and much lesser length. It was first waymarked as a Long Distance Route by National Park warden Richard Bell with help from local youth clubs and ramblers.

Alan Falconer published the first guidebook to the route in 1972, and clearly regarded his father as the creator of the Cleveland Way. Alec Falconer (1884-1968) had been a founder member of Middlesbrough Rambling Club in about 1907. Sadly he died just before the Way was finally opened, but there is a memorial plaque to him on Cringle Moor: see page 34.

In recent years, the trail has been managed by Natural England with funding mainly from government working in partnership with local councils and voluntary bodies. It has a full-time Route Manager, currently Malcolm Hodgson, based at the National Park HQ at the Old Vicarage, Bondgate, Helmsley, YO62 5BP; tel 01439 770 657. Email: **m.hodgson@ northyorkmoors-npa.gov.uk.**

Reading

Early guidebooks such as Alan Falconer's (HMSO 1972, 11-700329-8) and Bill Cowley's (Dalesman 1975, 0-85206-265-6) – both entitled *The Cleveland Way* – have historical interest and are available second-hand through specialist outlets.

Discover the North York Moors by Roger Osborne (NYM National Park Authority, 2007) 978-1-904622-13-0
This official guide to the National Park is informative, well illustrated and good value.

Useful websites

National Trail website
www.nationaltrail.co.uk/clevelandway
Essential first visit for walkers; rich resource, regularly updated

North York Moors National Park
www.northyorkmoors.org.uk
Great resource for learning more about natural history of the area; also has details of the Moorsbus service (operated at weekends April to October 2012)

Discover the Yorkshire Coast
www.discoveryorkshirecoast.com
Good tourism resource for the coastal section

Long Distance Walks Association
www.ldwa.org.uk/ldp
Compiles and maintains a database of long distance walks with pages on both the Cleveland Way and also the Tabular Hills Walk.

English Heritage
www.english-heritage.org.uk
Indispensable source on heritage: choose *Yorkshire and the Humber* for links to pages on Helmsley and Scarborough Castles, Mount Grace and Gisborough Priories and Rievaulx and Whitby Abbeys.

Accommodation

The official website
www.nationaltrail.co.uk/clevelandway
has two versions of its *Accommodation & Information Guide* – both are free to download and both are updated annually. The budget version lists campsites and hostels, the other lists hostels, B&Bs and hotels.

To book hostel accommodation directly, visit **www.yha.org.uk**: click *Yorkshire* for a map and list showing hostels at Helmsley, Osmotherley, Kildale (camping barn), Whitby, Boggle Hole and Scarborough.

Transport and weather

For national and local journey planning:

www.transportdirect.info
www.traveline.info
www.yorkshiretravel.net

Traveline can be phoned on 0871 200 2233.
For train information and tickets:

www.nationalrail.co.uk

For buses:

www.getdown.org.uk/bus
www.stagecoachbus.com
www.arrivabus.co.uk

For weather forecasts:

www.metoffice.gov.uk
www.bbc.co.uk/weather
or listen to local radio.

Holiday organisers and baggage carriers

The official website
www.nationaltrail.co.uk/clevelandway
has a section of service providers for walkers, including companies offering a full holiday package as well as baggage-only transfers.

Maps (printed and online)

We recommend (and sell at a discount from ***www.rucsacs.com***) Harvey's waterproof map *Cleveland Way* 978-185137489-2 which covers the whole route at a scale of 1:40,000 (2010 edition or later).

The Ordnance Survey *Explorer* series is at 1:25,000 and shows both Cleveland Way and Tabular Hills Walk. Two sheets (OL26, OL27) almost cover the route, but you need a third (301) to include Scarborough to Filey:

www.shop.ordnancesurveyleisure.co.uk

Visit our website for an online route map which lets you zoom for amazing detail and shows points of interest along the route:

www.rucsacs.com/routemap/cvw

Yorkshire words

Various local or dialect words are used in the Cleveland area and appear in the names of geographic features or places and villages. Here are some examples, with translations.

beck	stream, brook
brigg	headland or jetty
coble	traditional style of fishing boat
dale	valley
force, foss	waterfall
gill, ghyll	stream, ravine
howe	barrow or burial mound, usually round
nab	sharp drop at edge of a hill or plateau
rigg	ridge
scar or scaur	outcrop of rocks, esp flat rock at low tide
sea fret or roke	sea mist
sneck, snicket or ginnel	narrow alley (e.g. to prevent sheep from passing through)
wyke	bay, esp. with access to clifftop
yate	gate (pronounced **yatt**)

Countryside Code

The *Country Code* was first published for England & Wales in the 1950s and republished as the *Countryside Code* in 2012.
The leaflet is available for download from
www.naturalengland.org.uk
and this summary is taken from it (NE326):

Respect other people

- Consider the local community and other people enjoying the outdoors
- Leave gates and property as you find them and follow paths unless wider access is available

Protect the natural environment

- Leave no trace of your visit and take your litter home
- Keep dogs under effective control

Enjoy the outdoors

- Plan ahead and be prepared
- Follow advice and local signs

Notes for novices

Advice for novices is at *www.rucsacs.com* or send a suitably stamped envelope to us at Landrick Lodge, Dunblane, FK15 0HY.

Acknowledgements

We thank Trail Manager Malcolm Hodgson for his valuable comments on the manuscript, but are responsible for any errors that may remain. We thank him also for use of his overlay which we edited and enhanced for our online route map at *www.rucsacs.com/routemap/cvw*.

Feedback welcome

The publisher welcomes comments on this guidebook by email: **info@rucsacs.com**. The Trail Manager welcomes feedback on the trail: *m.hodgson@northyorkmoors-npa.gov.uk*.

Photo credits

The publisher thanks for permission to reproduce their copyright images: **Greg Johnson** 45 (middle); istockphoto.com/**Dan Kite** 18 (lower right); **Gordon Simm** front cover, title page, 4, 5, 7, 8 (all), 10, 13 (lower), 14, 17, 18 (upper and lower left), 19 (upper), 20 (both), 21 (all), 22 (both), 23 (both), 24, 25 (both) 26, 27 (both), 28, 29, 30 (both), 32, 33, 34 (all), 35, 36 (both), 37 (both), 40 (upper), 42 (both), 43, 44, 45 (lower), 47 (both), 48 (lower), 49, 50 (both), 51, 53, 54, 56 (both), 57 (both), 58, 59 (upper), 60 (both), back cover; **Jacquetta Megarry** 8 (lower), 13 (upper), 16 (lower), 19 (lower), 31, 38, 39, 40 (lower), 45 (upper), 46, 48 (upper), 52 (both), 55 (both), 59 (lower); **Detlef Thomas** 16 (upper).

Index